THE SIMPLE GUIDE TO
CUSTOMS AND ETIQUETTE
IN
ITALY

COVER ILLUSTRATIONS

FRONT: The Colosseum, the most famous relic of imperial
Rome, once the scene of gladiatorial combats.
BACK: Gondolas on the San Marco Canal with a view across
the water to St Mark's Basilica, Venice

ABOUT THE AUTHOR

HUGH SHANKLAND has spent 30 years visiting Italy and
teaching the language, history and culture. He is currently
Principal Lecturer in Italian Studies at the University of Durham,
England.

ILLUSTRATED BY
IRENE SANDERSON

THE SIMPLE GUIDE TO CUSTOMS AND ETIQUETTE IN

ITALY

HUGH SHANKLAND

GLOBAL BOOKS LTD

Simple Guides • Series 1
CUSTOMS & ETIQUETTE

The Simple Guide
CUSTOMS & ETIQUETTE IN ITALY
by Hugh Shankland

New edition 1996 by
GLOBAL BOOKS LTD
PO Box 219, Folkestone, Kent, England CT20 3LZ

© Global Books Ltd 1996

ISBN 1–86034–080–6

British Library Cataloguing in Publication Data
A CIP catalogue entry for this book
is available from the British Library

Distributed in the USA & Canada by:
The Talman Company, Inc, New York

Set in Futura 11 on 12 pt by Bookman, Slough
Printed in Great Britain by
The Cromwell Press Ltd., Broughton Gifford, Wiltshire

Contents

Introduction

Italy's best-known book on etiquette is called *Il Galateo*. It was written nearly 450 years ago at the height of the Renaissance by a Florentine priest called Monsignor Della Casa. A lot of the enduring appeal of his little manual lies in its amusing catalogue of 'don'ts'. For example, don't put your feet on the table when you eat. Don't walk off after dinner with your toothpick between your teeth like a bird making its nest. After blowing your nose don't open out your handkerchief and inspect the contents as though pearls and rubies had spilled out of your skull. Who can quarrel with such advice? And *Il Galateos*'s golden maxim is still as true as ever: 'Good manners depend on consideration of other people's wishes rather than your own pleasure.'

Della Casa was writing at a time when the sophisticated life of Italy's courts and patrician houses dictated the fashion for the rest of Europe, and foreign visitors used to cite the Italians' invention of the fork as the ultimate in refinement, when until then all the world had made do with fingers. Today, what constitutes good form is more or less standard throughout the western world, a watered down version of the conventions that prevailed when even Mussolini wore a bowler hat.

So *Customs and Etiquette in Italy* won't presume to lecture you on such matters as how to hold your fork in polite company in the land of pasta, though admittedly eating spaghetti without getting a chinful of sauce still presents problems even when armed with that indispensable invention. It just sets out to provide some basic information and advice for everyone who is interested not simply in visiting an astoundingly beautiful country but who is looking forward to enjoying the company of Italians and getting to know the way they choose to live.

The days may be gone when well-heeled Northern Europeans and Americans regarded a stay in Italy as a kind of obligatory finishing school for any half-way cultured young man or woman, and yet not a few visitors still discover that the Italians have something to pass on to others about the art of living.

I have been grateful for the opportunity to make substantial revisions and corrections for this expanded edition of a text originally published in 1991. A chapter 'On Business' has been added, and all sections have been updated in the light of social and political developments that in the past five years have made Italy an even more fascinating (and baffling) country to visit. Further tips on daily life in Italy can be found in the companion volume, *Very Simple Italian*.

H.S.
June 1996

ITALY

SWITZERLAND
Liechtenstein
VALLE
D'AOSTA
FRANCE
AUSTRIA
TRENTINO-
ALTO ADIGE
Milan
LOMBARDIA
FRIULI-
VENEZIA
GIULIA
Turin
PIEMONTE
VENETO
Venice
SLOVENIA
Trieste
Genoa
LIGURIA
EMILIA-
ROMAGNA
Bologna
YUGOSLAVIA
LIGURIAN
SEA
Pisa
Florence
TOSCANA
San Marino
MARCHE
BOSNIA-
HERZEGOVINA
CORSICA
(FRANCE)
Perugia
UMBRIA
LAZIO
ADRIATIC SEA
Vatican City
Rome
ABRUZZO
SARDINIA
MOLISE
Cagliari
CAMPANIA
Naples
TYRRHENIAN
SEA
Pompei
Capri
Sorrento
PUGLIA
BASILICATA
Bari
Brindisi
Cosenza
Catanzaro
IONIAN
SEA
CALABRIA
N
Marsala
Palermo
Messina
Reggio di Calabria
SICILY
Etna
TUNISIA
Agrigento
Catania
Syracuse
MEDITERRANEAN SEA

Land over 1000 metres
0   200km

8

1

Attitude to Foreigners

Venice

Italians are used to foreigners: pilgrims, merchants and invading armies in the past, armies of tourists today. Eight million people visit Venice every year, and there are only 75,000 Venetians. Being one of those eight million can make you feel like no more than another anonymous addition to the statistics of the tourist trade, and at times you will not be mistaken if you choose to interpret some unexpected courtesy towards you as another routine aspect of the nation's most lucrative industry.

On the other hand, such long familiarity with the presence of so many people from other countries means that over the centuries the Italians have come to be uncommonly tolerant of outsiders. A smile may very understandably conceal indifference but it will not mask hostility.

Besides, there are at least two very positive reasons for the general openness towards strangers. Hospitality is an ancient Mediterranean tradition, far from extinct even in the much accelerated pace of society today; furthermore, many Italians have close connections all over the world, not only through international trade and business contacts, but with their own kin, relatives and their descendants who were driven to emigrate in times when in many areas of Italy it was hard to make a decent living. Those times are over now. Italy is the fifth or sixth most prosperous of the world's largest industrialized nations, and one of the most vital and dynamic countries you will ever visit.

. . .the table is still the altar. . .

Rather than the land of immortal art and unspoilt nature projected by tourist brochures and sentimental films, Italy can strike the visitor as a very young country that is only just outgrowing its pioneering phase. In little over forty years it has come from an underdeveloped agricultural economy and small-town way of life to experience all the benefits and not a few of the drawbacks of newly affluent societies: greatly improved living standards, polluted rivers and seas, immigrant labour for the demeaning jobs, high crime rate, corrupt government, conspicuous consumption, sensationalist television, readily available drugs and porno.

In jaded moments one may reach the despairing conclusion that a gentle and almost virgin territory has been irredeemably violated by indiscriminate modernization driven by a get-rich-quick mentality blinded by consumer dreams. But there is abundant evidence that the superficial gloss has begun to tarnish, as the story of the Berlusconi empire illustrates, and everywhere one detects nostalgia for the good old days and ways.

There will be no need to go off the beaten track to find genuine warmth and disinterested attention. Visitors are frequently overwhelmed by the kindness they are shown, often from those who can least afford it. An old proverb in the Italian South says: 'A man doesn't go out to work his land when there's a festa, or bad weather, or friends in his home.'

'Prendiamo qualcosa?'

A chance meeting with an acquaintance swiftly progresses to 'Shall we have something?' (*Prendiamo qualcosa?*). On you walk together to the nearest bar, not to get tight but simply to mark the occasion with a little ceremony. And do not presume, by the way, that you will be allowed to pay for the Martinis or the two little espresso coffees. 'You can pay when I come to your country', is the most that might be conceded. But do offer just the same.

Spontaneous affability and agreeable informality characterize most Italians' direct dealings with outsiders. The popular image of

Italian men as slavish attenders on women is quite fallacious. There is little pointless gallantry: men do not feel obliged to open and shut doors for women getting in and out of cars for instance. Such formality as you encounter is most likely designed to put you at your ease. Communication counts so much more than form, and most people are quick to pick up on others' feelings and respond accordingly.

Language barriers are not seen as a formidable deterrent but as a challenge to use one's gifts of imagination and invention to make anyone uncomfortable feel at home, even if 'home' is only a railway compartment or a restaurant. Admittedly, you may meet with a very different experience if you come up against officialdom, but that is because not a few officials see the kind of formalities they handle as a test designed to try the patience of the people they are employed to serve. In such situations deference is a one-sided affair, only expected from you.

However, non-Italians do seem to enjoy a kind of unofficial diplomatic immunity, at least in the case of minor infringements such as traffic offences. If stopped by the very intimidating-looking traffic police you will probably be subjected to the routine of producing your papers for scrutiny, but you are unlikely to be fined. One thing that makes an official all-powerful in his little kingdom is the exercise of 'discretion'.

The English-speaking visitor has an extra bonus. English has never been more popular. In Milan alone there are said to be some seventy establishments which specialize in teaching English to adults. Proficiency in English, or a diploma alleging it, is regarded as a real career asset. 'Sport,' 'stress,' 'babysitter,' 'partner,' 'computer,' 'film,' 'trend,' 'jet-set' are just a few among hundreds of English words which crop up in everyday speech, and still more in the press and advertising. Some of the earliest anglicisms to be adopted suggest that certain supposedly typical English attitudes and customs seemed so eccentric to Italians that no native equivalents were felt to exist, viz. 'il relax', 'la privacy', 'l'understatement', 'l'hobby', 'il weekend'. Interestingly, these are all desirables cultivated by well-to-do Italians today. Graffiti such as 'I love Mario' and 'Juve is magic' testify to the universal appeal of English among the young who keenly follow the American and British pop scenes.

If it is nice to know that your language is appreciated why not return the compliment? After all, it is simple etiquette to learn at least a few phrases in the language of any country that

Graffiti

is host to you. For this reason some essential words and phrases are included at the end of this book, and occasionally in the text.

Italian is a particularly lovely language and luckily for the learner is pronounced more or less as it is written. There is no need to be shy about it. Your genuine efforts will not be mocked, and your mistakes will not be seized upon and pedantically corrected.

2

The Spice of Life: The Country, the People, the Climate

'There are twenty regions in Italy'

There are twenty regions in Italy. This is an administrative convenience, but also a reasonably accurate reflection of historical and cultural differences between each one of these regions. As a single nation, Italy only came into being at the will of a minority of politicians and patriots in the decade 1860–1870, little more than four generations ago. Until that time today's regions were mostly separate pieces in a jigsaw of independent kingdoms and duchies and city-states running from the Alps to Sicily.

With the significant exceptions of Piedmont in the north-west (the Kingdom of Savoy, under which the whole country eventually united) and the territory of the Church of Rome more or less in the centre of the peninsula, most of these states eventually succumbed to foreign rule. Each had its own distinct government and customs and vernacular. Centuries of wars and trade barriers fanned animosity toward neighbouring Italians, and strengthened local loyalties.

In attempting to weld these disparate entities into a single unified kingdom, Italy's early rulers created a heavily centralized state that was tailor-made for the nationalist dictator Mussolini to manipulate fifty years later. This over-centralized system run from Rome survived

Top Tip

If, today, a southerner strikes you as more ceremonial in speech and manner than his central or northern Italian counterpart this is partly because for over a thousand years the south, from Sicily to Naples, was influenced by the code of honour and elaborate etiquette of its Arab or Spanish rulers. If the paintings of the Florentine Renaissance look radically different from those of the same period in Venice this is just a clear reflection of the fact that Florence and Venice had quite independent histories, each resulting in a different sense of identity and contrasting philosophies of life.

fascism's downfall and the passing of the discredited monarchy. But it saddled the fledgling republic born out of the catastrophe of war with a huge and hugely inefficient bureaucracy, and antiquated mechanisms for decision-making that have handicapped the modernization of the country.

For half a century the state was administered, or misgoverned, by an increasingly corrupt more or less laissez-faire Catholic-liberal-socialist coalition or 'regime'. Since it was a powerful source of patronage, its excesses remained tolerated and unchecked until the early 1990s when scandalous revelations of boundless graft at all levels of politics and big business caused it to wither away almost overnight. To Italians its passing seemed as momentous as the disintegration of the Soviet empire. The 1996 elections, held after major electoral reforms, brought the ex-communists and their allies to power after fifty years in waiting.

Polarization between left and right appears as strong as ever in Italy, but the hope must be that the country will settle into a new era of responsible and effective government based at last on the democratic alternation in office of two major parties or political blocs.

Northern Italians' understandable anti-Rome sentiments have found a disquieting protest voice in a separatist party (*Lega del nord*) with impressively strong support in the prosperous and traditionally conservative north-east regions. In order to defuse its clamour for the break-up of united Italy the other major political forces could agree to remould the nation along federalist lines (on the German model) and so finally grant significant financial and executive independence to the regions. But this could make the economically strong North and Centre still richer, and the South yet poorer.

Despite the great social shake-up caused by the postwar 'economic miracle' which saw almost a third of the population relocate in search of work and better living conditions, the average Italian still tends to identify more strongly with his home region or even home village than with 'Italy', unless he is thinking of the national football team. In his view, genuine Italy and 'the best Italians' are found in his own small area of the nation: *'La Nazione'* (The Nation) is a paper serving only Tuscans!

This sort of micro-chauvinism is reinforced by the survival of strong linguistic differences: almost all Italians have a pronounced regional accent that makes their provenance quite easy to identify, and over half the population is still bilingual, i.e. fluent in a local dialect as well. The kind of Italian spoken in Piedmont sounds more than a bit like French, and nobody in mainland Italy understands the way people speak on the island of Sardinia. (Do not be alarmed, your own Italian will be understood everywhere. All Italians speak the 'national' brand of Italian that is used in every school in the land and in all branches of the media.)

Inevitably, given Italy's fragmented history, gaps in understanding exist on a deeper level than language. Many Italians appear less tolerant of some of their own compatriots than of the genuine foreigners in their midst. It is not at all rare to hear a northerner assert only half jokingly that 'Africa' begins south of Rome, and not a few would gladly include the capital itself.

Southerners resent the northerners' presumption of superiority, and champion what they see as their own capacity for greater human warmth and '*simpatia*'.

Real social and economic disparities do undeniably persist between north and south (where unemployment is persistently double the national average), but equally one often encounters a wilful failure to acknowledge the enormous material progress of the southern third of the country over the past half century. A modern communications system and vast improvements in the overall standard of living and levels of health and education now mean that there is really very little difference in the lifestyle of one Italian and the next, wherever they chance to live.

'*palio*' of Sienna

But regional pride and allegiance, this intense localism, has a very positive side to it too. It is the passion which keeps alive age-old traditions and festas, and assures that no amount of tourist promotion can turn genuine

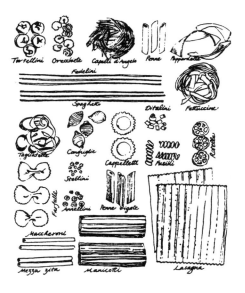

Pasta

popular participation in an event such as the *'palio'* of Siena or the *'regata storica'* of Venice into a soulless charade. It also guarantees the survival of a flourishing and wonderfully varied regional cuisine. Italians, who eat out more than any other population in Europe, will travel far to search out authentic local dishes.

Top Tip

Italy's rich regional diversity explains why there are over 2,000 different names for a bewildering variety of pasta shapes, or why the country produces more brands of wine – at least 4,000 – than anywhere else in the world.

The visitor, too, will find that in Italy variety is literally the spice of life: butter and rice and black pepper in northern cooking, abundant oil and pasta and hot red pepper in the south. Scented truffle grated over your spaghetti in Piedmont, a sauce of crushed basil and pine nuts in Liguria, and of fresh sardines in Sicily.

The climate, like the population, is much more varied than is often assumed. Temperatures in northern Italy are on average four degrees cooler than in the south, because the country extends over ten degrees of latitude. If you were to drive from top to toe you would travel some 1,400 kilometres, along the excellent national motorway (*autostrada*) system, from the Brenner pass on the same latitude as Berne in Switzerland down to Sicily on the same latitude as Tunis.

Despite its long coastline the country is very mountainous, only a quarter is lowland. The towering Alps and Dolomites fringe the whole of the northern region, and the Appenine mountain chain runs like a backbone down the length of the peninsula from the Gulf of Genoa to the Straits of Messina, with peaks covered in snow until early summer.

The inhabitants of Milan, in the great northern plain of the river Po, have to endure winters as cold as Copenhagen with an airport that registers an average of 100 days of fog per year, yet the summers are almost as hot as Naples, without its refreshing sea breezes. Turin, the other great northern city, is even chillier in winter but its position at the foot of the Alps gives it less torrid summer days.

Coastal areas are everywhere dry and hot in summer, but subject also to violent thunderstorms which can cause sudden drastic flooding. Inland cities such as Florence and Rome are delightful early in the year but can be unpleasantly heavy and sticky in July and especially August, even at night.

August is the crazy month in Italy and the worst time to visit unless all you crave is a deckchair in the sun. The whole country is on holiday apart from those servicing the holiday-makers. This is no time to do business. Offices and factories and government departments are shut and all have fled to cool off at the seaside or in the hills and mountains. Historic towns erected centuries before the motor-car are for once a delight for the pedestrian, but it is less gratifying for the visitor to find the majority of shops and restaurants and some of the most important museums closed and public transport unreliable. Towards the end of the third week, after the 'ferragosto' national holiday, life returns gradually to normal. Fierce cloudbursts break the long heatwave and a suntanned population drifts back to its homes and jobs.

Florence

Spring and early summer and autumn are the best times for comfortable sightseeing, though in Easter week major tourist centres like Rome and Florence and Venice are packed to capacity, and throughout April and May you can expect to share the sights and sites with crowds of Italian schoolchildren on excursions. September and early October, when hotel rates and plane fares are cheaper, are often especially beautiful with clear fresh sunny days at the time of the grape harvest. But be warned, October and November are on average the wettest months of the year. Winter is the time for the opera-goer and the skier, and the Christmas shopper in Rome, but before the end of February pink almond is blossoming in the extreme south.

'la passeggiata'

One of the great delights of Italy is how much of life is lived outdoors, at least in the warm half of the year. All the larger towns have more or less permanent outdoor markets, and every village has its lively market day. In summer, theatres and opera houses and the majority of cinemas shut their doors. Entertainment moves outside, with open-air feasting and dancing, string quartets in palace courtyards, films under the stars, rock concerts and opera in city parks and ancient amphitheatres. This is the season for a thousand local festas and festivals.

Wet summers do happen, even in Italy. Whatever time you go, pack a light waterproof at the very least, and also light boots and strong walking shoes. A collapsible umbrella could prove useful.

3

The Family, Men and Women

'Children'

In this Catholic country that shares its capital with the Vatican City, large families are a thing of the past. Italy now has both the lowest birthrate in Europe and one of its most long-lived populations, so that there are now three grandparents to every grandchild. In the reforming 1970s divorce and abortion were legalized with the support of the majority of the population. However, despite alarmist cries about a 'crisis of the family,' the family is still Italy's most solid institution. Myriad small family businesses form the backbone of the nation's economy.

The remarkably low rate of divorce (five times lower than the UK) must show that preservation of the family unit is more important than marital compatibility or fidelity. Children (not only one's own) are even more idolized now that they are so relatively rare, and when small are expensively dressed as miniature adults. All the same, although welcome everywhere they are not specially catered for: children's menus are unknown in restaurants and nappy changing facilities are unheard of.

When grown up, sons and daughters normally go on living at home until they marry, and sometimes long after, though this is also a reflection of a long-standing national housing crisis and rising youth unemployment. In 1996 an astonishing 40% of males between 25 and 34 were still living with their parents. Again, if youngsters choose to study, as a very high proportion do, they tend to live at home and attend the nearest university. Such a supportive and protective upbringing seems to encourage self-confident and secure personalities although, inevitably, 'mammismo' (Mummy's boy syndrome) is common.

Women are still expected to fulfil their traditional roles of housewife and cook and mamma, but increasingly also to be wage-earners. The economic demands of the consumer society have thus only partially liberated them from home and the stove, although strikingly progressive legislation has helped to ensure, at least in theory, that they are no longer regarded as man's inferiors. The typical Italian male notoriously used to categorize women as either madonnas or whores, mothers or mistresses. Such caveman attitudes still exist – where do they not? – but today's greater social and sexual fredoms mean that relations between men and women are much more humane and relaxed, especially among the young. Macho images and Latin lover stereotypes are more likely to be ridiculed than applauded.

The popular press often features articles about Italian males supposedly 'in crisis', fearful for their ego and fertility in the face of self-confident 'new women' high achievers. The threat does not seem that great: a recent survey concluded that only 8% of the country's top people were women. However, 62% of these were single, and 74% of those who were married had no children.

'Church wedding . . . the done thing'

Church attendance may have declined dramatically, but a church wedding with all the trappings is still very much the done thing, and 80% of the population declare themselves to be believers. Broadly Catholic attitudes, in particular the prioritizing of family interests, still count enormously. The benign outlook that regards us all as sinners but none of us beyond redemption might go some way towards explaining why man-made rules and regulations are often more honoured in the breach than the observance. Not only the flesh is weak: no one is particularly shocked by misdeeds like tax evasion (officially estimated at 90% in the case of the self-employed) and house-construction in contravention of building regulations (recognized to be millions of dwellings). Governments regularly pardon such universal sins by decreeing mass amnesties in return for simple confession of wrongdoing and payment of a token fine.

No doubt, in the fullness of time, a similar blanket pardon will arrive for all those hundreds of prominent personalities suspected of corruption in the '*Mani pulite*' (Clean Hands) blitz on graft. . . Tolerance and forgiveness are built into the legal system itself, which offers even assassins lenient treatment if they recant and turn informer. But an important benefit of the *pentiti* (repentants) system is that it has enabled the authorities to recruit hundreds of self-confessed *mafiosi* to help them fight the mafia. The mafia itself, as many have pointed out, thrives on a brutal parody of ancient and admirable southern virtues of family solidarity and loyalty to one's friends.

In certain villages, particularly in the south, you may still find the traditional separation into male and female spheres but all in all Italian wives and daughters are no more possessively 'protected' by husbands and fathers than in any other advanced industrialized society.

Having said this, a foreign woman on her own can still have a tiresome time. The best way to avoid the feeling of being hunted is just to be yourself, be natural and open in the company of people who act in the same way, and simply ignore anyone who treats you any other way, no matter how irritated or insulted you feel. As at home, most of this is just bravado, to preserve one's standing with the other lads.

'. . .using any language. . .'

4

Dress

'la bella figura'

In a country which boasts so many of the world's leading fashion houses and where individuals can be so assertive, it is perhaps surprising that Italians are not less conventional dressers. But at all levels *'la bella figura'*, i.e. looking good and making a good impression, is a high priority, and there is quite a lot of snobbery over turn-out. Most people spend their money on smart rather than showily modish gear, and even those with a strong penchant for self-display tend to opt for expensive but safe 'labels'. In their time, Milan's punks were surely the most immaculate in Europe.

All this simply means that, as with so much else in contemporary Italy, style and taste or more accurately expense and image ('*il look*'!) are what you are judged by. Styles for both men and women lay great emphasis on the quality of material as well as cut. Fashionable men tend to affect a vaguely 'English' look: tweed jackets and corduroy trousers, or a dark blue blazer with darkish trousers in winter, lighter in summer. The latter combination would be suitable for the office, or of course a smart suit. Great care is taken over the selection of shirt and tie, and good shoes. Men are not afraid of wearing scent, and without feeling their masculinity is in any way diminished may carry a leather handbag ('*il borsello*') which among other things can come in handy for the increasingly ubiquitous mobile phone. Jackets soon come off in summer. Only a few of the very classiest restaurants will insist on ties being worn.

Women generally go for a tastefully glamorous look, with particular attention to their hair and the styling of shoes and handbag. An expensive silk blouse and figure-flattering long pants set off by a striking belt and shoes is a common combination. Tailored suits are favourites for formal wear. Leather goods and garments are very popular and of high quality. Costume jewellery, large earrings, gold necklaces and bracelets are widely worn, and often ornamentation is very conspicuous. For evening wear a black dress is a popular solution, again with carefully selected accessories and probably a rather special brooch. Despite a growing animal rights movement, Italian women show no inhibitions about wearing real animal furs, indeed fur coats are extraordinarily popular.

As for casual wear, sports clothes are immensely popular with both men and women, whether or not they ever wield a tennis racket or jog round the park. An American rather than French or British look prevails: baseball caps, colourful tracksuits, designer sweatshirts and trainers. Jeans are worn almost universally, and by all ages. At the seaside and in seaside towns in summer anything goes, barring total nudity.

Even if travelling in the hot months bring a light jacket or shawl or cardigan for the cool of the evening. Since the Italians are so clothes-conscious, men as well as women receive compliments if they take the trouble to dress well.

Top Tip

The Church has finally relented on the question of women and clothing, or at least to the extent of no longer insisting that hair is covered. But men as well as women may still be barred from entering a church if wearing shorts or a top that leaves the shoulders bare.

5

Social Occasions & Situations

'If in doubt: shake'

When to shake hands? Always when introduced or introducing yourself, and when taking your leave. This means you can shake hands with the same person twice in thirty seconds: if a friend introduces you to an acquaintance of his in the street you will shake hands again before parting, even if not a word has passed between you. Two colleagues headed in opposite directions will momentarily clasp hands as they walk past each other without even dropping their speed.

When new arrivals enter the room in a fairly formal situation such as the start of a party, even if they are well-known to everyone all the men present will rise and shake hands. Women remain seated, unless an elderly or very special person has come in. A man might give a woman a kiss on the back of the hand, just a graceful compliment if done without affectation.

Two kisses, one on each cheek (commonly the left first then the right) is the norm between relatives and close acquaintances when meeting or parting. Children, of course,

'. . .a graceful compliment'

are much hugged and kissed. Good friends embrace freely, men as well. Men are seen walking arm in arm almost as much as women. It is good to renew contact. Friendship is precious, something worth demonstrating, even advertising.

What sort of things do people say? *'Piacere'* means 'Nice to meet you.' *'Ciao'* is 'hello' (and also 'goodbye') but is normally only used when you know someone well. On meeting others you would say *'buon giorno'* or *'buona sera'* ('good day' or 'good evening'). There is no 'good afternoon,' so *'buona sera'* is used from about five o'clock on. A woman is addressed as *'Signora'* whether or not she is married, and a girl is *'Signorina.'* But *'Signore,'* the term of address for a man, unless coupled with the man's surname is only used by a person in a service role, a waiter or a shop assistant for instance (cf. English 'Sir').

In addressing men in business and professional contexts there is much resort to titles: *'dottore'* (doctor, but also in theory anyone with a university degree), *'ingegnere'* (engineer), *'ragioniere'* (accountant), *'professore'* (any teacher above elementary school level) etc. Women professionals are similarly addressed: *'dottoressa,'* *'professoressa'* etc. In the South this respect for titles can be excessive, and in quite ordinary situations anyone with the smallest degree of social standing can be honoured with at least *'dottore'*! (For other expressions of greeting etc. see Useful Words & Phrases, p.60.)

If you receive an invitation it is normal to answer by telephone partly because the mail is appallingly inefficient. It is customary to arrive with a bunch of flowers or a box of chocolates for your hostess, though flowers can be sent round in advance or delivered as a 'thank you' the next day. It is not done to bring a bottle, except perhaps champagne if there is some special cause for celebration.

As regards the old-time 'language of flowers,' all that everyone agrees on these days is that red roses signify 'passion' and are sent in bunches of a dozen. Beyond that all is confusion, as some say yellow roses mean 'jealousy', others 'friendship.' Pink is safe. Flowers (except red roses) should be in odd numbers: 5, 7, 9 etc.

Twelve red roses

As for other taboos, there is ambivalence over the number 13. Thirteen at table is definitely to be avoided, but many declare 13

Top Tip

When buying flowers as a gift you must remember: never give chrysanthemums. In Italy they are the flowers of the dead; they belong on coffins and graves. For similar reasons, white lilies are never given to a couple with children.

to be a lucky number for them, as it is for the lottery in Naples, and Naples is the most superstitious city in Italy. 17 is the unluckiest number, and Tuesday or particularly Friday 17th are very bad days. 'Neither on a Friday nor a Tuesday get married or start a journey,' runs a very popular saying. And many add: 'Or do business,' i.e. clinch a deal.

Italians of all classes tend to be superstitious, at least to some extent. Fortune-tellers advertise widely and one of the three national TV channels transmits a daily 'horoscope' for viewers, read by a bearded and beaded astrologer. Many commonly-held superstitions will be familiar to you, others less so: a black cat crossing your path is a most sinister omen, never sleep in a bed with its foot facing the door, do not put a hat on a bed, do not break a mirror, spill salt or oil, or pour wine 'backwards' with your hand held under the bottle, and do not place a loaf or bread roll upside down.

Luckily, there is an instant remedy: make the devil's horn sign with your right hand (it is bad luck with the left!): jab your hand at the ground with forefinger and little finger projected, or better still touch metal (not wood) with the same two fingers. It will be a good year for you if the first person you see on New Year's morning is a man, a bad year if it is a woman. It must be progress that another version is now more generally accepted: it will bring good luck if the person you see is of the opposite sex to yourself.

Smoking is likely to be more of a danger to you than any of the above. It is banned in all public places, including the subway, and 'Vietato fumare' (smoking forbidden) is one of the few injunctions that Italians almost invariably observe. Which is impressive, as large numbers are still quite heavy smokers. If you fall into the same category yourself, rest assured that it is all right at the end of a meal to ask if anyone minds if you smoke. The odds are that half the table will light up gratefully. In restaurants you may be asked politely to put out a cigarette, although larger premises have a *'settore per fumatori'* (smokers' section).

'panettone'

In the case of a meal among close friends or relatives someone will generally arrive bearing a big cake or whatever from a pastry shop as dessert. Another might bring a quality

Top Tip

'Service' is automatically incorporated in restaurant bills but since the waiter himself does not get it all it is normal to leave another 5% or so if you feel you have been well attended. In hotels, porters and doormen will expect a small gratuity, and the same goes for room service. Chambermaids should be handsomely tipped if you have stayed several days. Taxi drivers will expect 10% of the fare. In bars, it is common practice to present a 100 or 200-lire coin for the barman along with the tab for your drink.

wine. At Christmas-time almost no one calls without a large boxed *'panettone'* or some other delicacy associated with the season. Extravagant presents of baskets and hampers of food and wine and spirits are given by companies at Christmas or New Year to business associates and good clients. Other commercial 'homages', as they are known, include lavishly-produced company calendars, cut glass, glossy coffee-table publications, inscribed fountain pens etc. Easter eggs get bigger and gaudier by the year.

'. . .a delicacy'

Every town has one or two shops that specialize in supplying the conventional gifts that go with big family occasions such as weddings, christenings, and first communion (for boys and girls around eight or nine, who are much-feted in their smart white outfits). Each guest brings a suitable gift and is in turn presented with a souvenir *'bomboniera,'* i.e. a ceramic or cut-glass bowl or sweetbox containing sugared almonds, again in odd numbers, wrapped in white tulle. Anyone unable to come receives the sugared almonds through the post. Expenditure on the clothes and food is lavish. The celebratory feast can last all afternoon and is normally held in a large restaurant. Some families celebrate a name-day ('*onomastico*,' the saint's day corresponding to a person's own name) in grander style than a birthday.

Obviously, in your case it will be appreciated if you give things from your own country as presents. For example, English china and Scottish woollens are very popular.

6

Food and Drink

'. . .at the dinner table. . .'

Traditionally, the main meal of the day is lunch ('*il pranzo*'). Breakfast ('*la prima colazione*') is strictly speaking not a meal at all, and if you are staying in a hotel it is hardly worth the extra expense for just a can of coffee and bread and jam. Much better to go to a local bar like half the rest of the population and order a delicious '*cappuccino*' (coffee with hot frothy milk) and a '*pasta*,' which in this case means pastry, a doughnut or a custard-filled croissant etc.

The lunch-time break for most offices and businesses is at least two hours, so the whole family can be reunited. The children are back home too, as school hours are generally only mornings, from 8.30 to 12.30, but include Saturdays.

A plentiful supply of bread (without butter) accompanies every meal, and there will always be wine on the table and bottled mineral water. The head of the household will pour the first round of wine and perhaps propose a personal or general toast (*'brindisi'*), and after that all look after themselves. Sometimes, wine is not poured until after the

'In the middle of the day. . .'

43

pasta course. Italy produces some very choice wines, but generally no great fuss is made of the wine, which is just a natural accompaniment to any meal.

A full-scale *'pranzo'* is very substantial. Most families would only treat themselves to it on a Sunday or when eating out. Two main course dishes are preceded by a starter, and followed by fruit, cheese and dessert. The starter or *'antipasto'* might be an hors d'oeuvre of cold meats and marinated vegetables for instance, or melon and Parma ham. The first main dish (*'primo piatto'* or simply *'primo'*) will be pasta or risotto (rice dish) or soup (*'minestra'*). The second main dish (*'secondo piatto'* or *'secondo'*) will be fish or meat (often two or three varieties – there are very few vegetarians in Italy!), plus a vegetable or salad as a side dish (*'contorno'*).

Celeriac salad with Parma ham

Potatoes do not automatically accompany meat or fish, though chips (*'patatine'*) can always be ordered in a restaurant. There is generally only one side dish and it may arrive after the 'secondo piatto' has been consumed, salad being regarded as a palate-cleanser after richer food. Note that pasta on its own (except perhaps in the case of lasagne) is not considered a meal in itself, whereas a pizza is, and they come in all sizes. If you feel a whole pasta dish before the 'secondo' will be too much for the children or yourself it is quite in order to ask for a half portion ('mezza porzione') in a restaurant.

People usually linger long at the dinner table, with plenty of conversation accompanying the leisurely consumption of cheese (eaten with knife and fork, not on bread or biscuits) and fresh fruit and dessert. As the meal draws to a close there is often animated debate about other marvellous meals people have had, and their favourite dishes. It is not felt to be bad form! No 'pranzo' would be complete without coffee, but many decline it after an evening meal claiming they do not sleep well after coffee. After the meal you may be offered a liqueur, grappa or sambuca, or an 'amaro' or 'digestivo', bitter-sweet aromatic syrupy concoctions that are meant to settle a full stomach.

A buffet meal ('pranzo in piedi') is something that has caught on as a convenient way of coping with larger numbers of guests than can be squeezed round a dinner table. Chic households may issue invitations for a 'cocktail', but this is more typical for official functions, or a vernissage etc.

A vermouth or a chilled light white wine such as Pinot or Verduzzo is often taken as an 'aperitivo' before sitting down to a good meal. In the late evening brandy or grappa or whisky may be produced, but glasses will be infrequently filled. Few Italians are hard drinkers, as

Monsieur Della Casa was gratified to note as long ago as 1555: 'I thank God that for all the many other plagues that have come to us from beyond the Alps, this most pernicious custom of making game of drunkenness, and even admiring it, has not yet reached as far as this' (*Il Galateo*).

'. . . acquiring your pitch'

Top Tip

First-time visitors to Italy be warned: If you sit at a table ('*al tavolo*') in a bar with waiter service whether inside or out on the pavement the cost of a drink is up to three times higher than if taken standing ('*al banco*'). In the latter case, you generally pay for your order first at the cash desk ('*la cassa*') and present your receipt ('*scontrino*') to the barman specifying what you have paid for. In smaller family-run establishments it is more normal to pay after. However, there is one great advantage of the *al tavolo* option: once you have bought your drink you have acquired a pitch from which you will come under no pressure to move on. You can sit for hours writing postcards or just watching the world go by.

Alcohol consumption is high, one of the highest levels in Europe, but it is spread evenly among the population and most people's intake is confined to a couple of glasses of wine at mealtimes, even then very often diluted with water. As a rule, an Italian does not need to have a drink in his hand to feel comfortable at a party, or to down several cocktails before starting to feel 'good'. Partly for this reason older people shake their heads at the vogue among youngsters for driving hundreds of miles for all-night raves at fashionable discos, where they can get high on alcohol or Ecstasy.

7

Out & About

'There is no queuing. . .'

Shops are generally open in the morning between 9.00 am and 1.00 pm, though many close by 12.30 and food stores may open as early as 8.00 am, by which time markets are also doing lively business. In the middle of the day there is a three-hour lunch and siesta break after which shops open for a further four hours from 3.30 or 4.00 until 7.30 or 8.00 in the evening. Many smaller shops close all Saturday afternoon. There is as yet very little Sunday opening except in the build-up to Christmas and in holiday resorts during the high season.

Except for the big stores, all shops have half-day closing during the week, generally

Top Tip

Bargaining is the norm at markets other than food stalls, and small shops may also be ready to oblige if you are bold enough to ask for a discount (*'sconto'*). No one will think the worse of you, not even if a notice saying *'Prezzi fissi'* (no bargaining) is displayed.

Monday. Bars and restaurants close for one day in seven, usually mid-week. Barbers and hairdressers are open all day Saturday and closed all day Monday. At least one 24-hour chemist (*'farmacia'*) is open seven days a week in every sizeable city. (For business working hours see chapter 8.)

Bank opening times are best checked locally, as hours of business vary considerably. Generally speaking, all banks open mornings from about 9.00 am to about 1.30 pm, Monday to Friday only. Most also open for a single hour in mid-afternoon, earlier in the north and centre of the country (e.g. 2.30–3.30), later in the south (e.g. 3.30–4.30). International credit cards are accepted in quality hotels and restaurants and shops. If you need cash out of banking hours, an exchange bureau (*'cambio'*) will operate the same hours as shops and they are located in city centres and at stations and airports. Hotels will always change travellers' cheques, though not necessarily at the most favourable rate. Bank cash dispensers are very temperamental, especially after 9.00 pm, and often do not recognize cards other than their own.

Museum opening hours vary widely, with some closing as early as noon and others as late as 2.00 pm – by no means all open again before the following morning.

Many have free admission one day a week. Note that nearly all museums are closed on Mondays, including popular archaeological sites such as Pompeii. Churches open early for mass but are generally shut between midday and late afternoon.

Public toilets are few and far between, but almost every bar has one, and in Italy a bar is never far away. Standards of hygiene are usually tolerable. Do not be shy about walking in and asking for 'il gabinetto' or 'la toelette'. You will not be expected to buy a drink or an ice-cream in return for the favour, but it would be appreciated.

'alimentari'

Traffic can look very daunting if you have to cross the road. Do not be alarmed when you find the cars will not stop for you if you wait patiently on the kerb at the appropriate crossing. No law obliges them to halt if there is nothing in front of them. They will stop or alter course when they see that otherwise they would hit a pedestrian, which is logical. So choose your moment well and step out boldly, making your intention plain. Since this is the system, drivers are used to responding quickly, fortunately. In theory, jay-walkers can be fined for not using pedestrian crossings.

'Traffic can look very daunting'

Local buses and trams have a very low flat fare (e.g. 1200 lire), and in some big cities the ticket is valid for an hour or more from when you first board, so it can be used for more than one ride. Tickets are sold singly or in books of ten in bars and at tobacconists ('*tabacchi*') and news-stands along main routes and when you board you insert your ticket in a machine which punches it with the time and date. All-day visitors' tickets may be had too.

In places like Rome or Naples it can seem to you that everyone else has a valid season ticket or believes that only mugs do not take free rides. Seats are few. On crowded buses beware of pickpockets. Work your way up to the exit in good time before your stop. Two invaluable words: '*Permesso*' (Excuse me) and '*Scendo*' (I am getting off at this stop).

The same two words will come in handy at rush-hour on the subway ('*metropolitana*'). There are expanding networks in Milan, Genoa, Rome and Naples, and more under construction in other major towns. The subway (in many sections overground) is cheap and fast, but in all cases except Milan the lines only cover very limited areas of the city and suburbs. Scooters and motorbikes are making a big comeback, as cities have got so congested.

If you take a taxi make sure the meter is running at the start of the journey. In southern cities there are many unofficial cabs and moonlighters. If you have to use one, negotiate a (fair) price before you set out.

There will soon be one car for every two inhabitants in Italy. Only Venice and the peaceful hill-towns of Tuscany and Umbria where motorists have to park outside the city walls are havens for the pedestrian. Most cities have declared traffic-free zones and no-parking areas in some parts of their historic centres, but this only increases the pressure elsewhere.

Florence is one of the worst cities for traffic congestion, and in Rome cars would park on top of each other if they could. In cities, it is best to park your car wherever you can and proceed on foot or by bus. Never leave anything inside a car visible to a thief, and take the car radio with you if possible. Note that most service stations not on motorways close over lunch, and many do not open on Sundays.

For drivers in Italy Monsignor Della Casa's golden maxim (see page 6!) does not apply. As in the case of queuing, 'me first' is the rule, and unless you want to risk causing an accident through your extreme courtesy or reverence for the highway code you should join the crowd in the spirit of a rather better-known maxim: When in Rome. . .

Sometimes you may think all drivers act as though they are driving dodgems, but on the whole the Italian is a skilful driver. He (and she) may seem over-keen to prove it, but remember the intention is always to dodge, not bump. Fines are heavy but no one observes speed limits unless they happen to spot a speed camera.

Buon viaggio!

8

On Business

'Il made in Italy'

It can be a singular pleasure to do business in Italy. Contrary to ancient prejudices about unreliability and lack of punctuality and so on, you will find Italy's manufacturers and entrepreneurs and middlemen are very able and efficient practitioners of the skills of production and promotion, and well used to thinking internationally. *Il made in Italy* is how Italians term the combination of high quality product and design and export acumen which has been such a remarkable success story ever since the 'economic miracle' of the late 1950s, most notably in the case of the go-ahead family firm that typifies the Italian business scene.

Business can be a social pleasure, too, as contacts will want to take time out to get to know their opposite numbers better, usually through the medium of fairly long and leisurely meals in excellent restaurants where relaxing together is not just part of the softening up process. If this seems to be a waste of precious time during a short business trip, you will find it amply compensated by a willingness to work unusually long if flexible hours when under pressure. People in positions of responsibility can be on the premises as early as 7.00 am and still be around far into the evening. All the same, when planning a business trip you will need to take account of normal Italian business hours and the shape of the working year.

Government offices only operate a half-day schedule: 8.30 or 9.00 am until 1.30 or 2.00 pm (very convenient for the thousands of state employees who augment their rather modest earnings by taking a second job). Dealing with the sort of formalities that will take you to government offices can be a very slow and trying experience, so start in as early as you can. For anyone planning a longer stay, such apparently routine operations as trying to open a bank account, or procuring a *carta di soggiorno* or getting a telephone installed can turn out to be anything but simple and straightforward.

'Mediterranean lunchbreak'

Small and medium-size firms throughout the country still generally observe the long Mediterranean lunchbreak, working 9.00 am– 1.00 pm and then 3-7.00 pm, but more and more are changing over to the standard 9 to 5 office schedule (*orario americano*), although this is still very rare in southern Italy.

Apart from Christmas Day and Boxing Day, New Year's Day, Easter Monday, and the long August vacation, national holidays in the working calendar are:

    6 January (Epiphany)
    25 April (Liberation Day)
    1 May (Labour Day)
    2 June (Republic Day)
    1 November (All Saints)
    8 December (Immaculate Conception)

If on some other day no one answers your call this could be because there is some purely local holiday to honour the patron saint of the town, or because the whole office has taken a *ponte*, a 'bridge' day off between a national holiday and *il weekend*.

In face-to-face negotiation you will have the advantage that English will be assumed to be the lingua franca, but relatively few Italians are particularly confident in English so will probably avail themselves of at least the token

Top Tip

Remember that for the whole of the month of August virtually all businesses close down entirely, and government offices if open will only be manned by a skeleton staff. The last days in July will be marked by a slowing down process in anticipation of the big August break.

services of an interpreter. If you hope to impress personally, you can cut a *bella figura* yourself by investing in the much admired best quality English men's suits and shoes. For women, a smart dress sense is of course particularly appreciated.

Even if initiating your side of the correspondence in English you can expect to receive replies in Italian from the smaller firms. Commercial and bureaucratic Italian are terminologies all of their own, and it might be advisable to turn to a translation agency to decipher them.

The classic Gambalonga

Since the country's postal system is notoriously slow and unreliable, the advent of faxing facilities has been a great asset for Italian business efficiency and companies are now of course increasingly taking advantage of e-mail.

Transport and airport workers' snap strikes are a hazard to travellers with little time on their hands, particularly in June and July when annual contracts are up for negotiation. There are good fast and reliable inter-city trains that are relatively inexpensive, and the frequent north-south internal flights are very valuable services. Remember, some airports (e.g. Milan, Rome and Venice) can be quite a long way out of town, and Florence airport is actually at Pisa!

9

Some Useful Words & Phrases

You only need to bear in mind a few points in order not to seriously mispronounce a word. Consonants **'c'** and **'g'** are pronounced soft before 'e' and 'i': **'ce'** as in 'chest,' **'ge'** as in 'gentle,' **'ci'** as in 'chill,' **'gi'** as in 'gin.' On the other hand **'ch'** and **'gh'** are hard: **'ch'** as in 'kilo' (Italian: 'chilo'), **'che'** as in 'Kent,' **'ghi'** as in 'give,' **'ghe'** as in 'get.' **'sce'** is pronounced as in 'shell' and **'sci'** as in 'ship.' **'gn'** is like the first 'n' in 'onion.' **'gl'** sounds like the 'll' in 'million.'

sì, no	yes, no
per favore/per piacere	please
grazie/grazie mille	thanks/ thanks a lot
prego	you're welcome
molto gentile	very kind of you
buon giorno	good morning/afternoon
buona sera	good evening
buona notte	good night
scusi	excuse me
posso presentare. . .	may I introduce. . .
piacere	nice to meet you
mi chiamo. . .	my name is. . .
parla inglese?	do you speak English?
mi dispiace	I'm sorry
non capisco	I don't understand
arrivederci/ci vediamo	goodbye/see you again
auguri!	good luck! best wishes!
salute!	cheers!
ha una camera singola/ doppia?	do you have a single/ double room?
per une notte/due/tre notti	for one night/two/three nights
con doccia, con bagno	with shower, with bath
quanto costa?	how much is it?
dove	where
dov'é il bagno?	where's the toilet/bathroom
quando	when
quando arriva/parte?	when does it arrive/leave?
a che ora apre/chiude?	what time does it open/ close?
alle tre e un quarto	at a quarter past three
alle quattro e mezzo	at half past four
alle sei meno cinque	at five minutes to six
buon appetito	enjoy your meal
buona giornata	have a good day
buona fortuna	good luck
buon divertimento	have a nice time
buon viaggio	have a good trip

10

Did You Know?

'The world's artistic heritage'

Italy is a land of paddy fields, tobacco plantations, and volcanoes: the rice fields are in Piedmont, tobacco flourishes in Puglia, and Italy has Europe's only two active volcanoes: mighty Mount Etna in Sicily, and the remote volcanic island of Stromboli. Vesuvius last erupted in 1944.

According to a UNESCO report over 50% of the world's artistic heritage is concentrated in Italy. Recently restored supreme masterpieces of painting are Michelangelo's Sistine Chapel ceiling and 'Last Judgement' in the Vatican, Leonardo da Vinci's 'Last Supper' in Milan, Piero della Francesca's fresco cycle of the 'True Cross' in Arezzo, and Masaccio's 'Stories of St Peter' frescos in the Chiesa del Carmine, Florence.

A single northern region, Lombardy (main city Milan), accounts for 20% of Italy's GDP. Average incomes in the country's poorest area, the southernmost mainland region of Calabria, are only half those of Lombardy.

There are two mini-states within Italy's borders: Vatican City, the tiniest state in the world (108 acres), and San Marino (23 square miles), the oldest extant republic in the world, dating from the 4th century AD.

The Colosseum in Rome was built to hold 50,000 spectators. Even now, on a summer's night, you can join 25,000 spectators in the 1st-century Arena of Verona, one of the largest and best-preserved Roman amphitheatres, for a performance of Verdi's *Aida* or Puccini's *Turandot*. The spectacular ruins of ancient Rome's most luxurious public baths, the Baths of Caracalla, are the setting for the summer opera season in the capital.

Some of the most impressive monuments of the civilization of ancient Greece are actually in Italy: the temples at Paestum (south of Naples), and in Sicily the great theatre of Syracuse, and the temples at Agrigento, Selinunte and Segesta.

Christians have been making their way to Rome ever since St Peter and St Paul. The official estimate of the number of pilgrims expected in Rome for the *Anno Santo*, Jubilee year 2000, is 40 million! Enormous sums of money have been allocated for the restoration of historic sites and buildings, galleries, parks, the riverside, transport and road systems, to give the Eternal City a much-needed facelift. Needless to say, I am postponing my pilgrimage until the year 2001!

'quanto costa?'